I0421214

Pillars of Wealth

A Blueprint for Building Lasting Financial Well-Being

Jordan Penix

About the Author

Jordan Penix is a prominent author, financial expert, and entrepreneur, whose  trajectory in the world of finance has been driven by a tireless quest for knowledge and a love for empowering people. Holding a Bachelor's degree in Finance, Jordan's educational background is the base of his thorough comprehension of financial fundamentals.

With a career spanning over a decade, Jordan has successfully navigated the nuances of the financial business, obtaining hands-on expertise in areas such as investment management, financial planning, and entrepreneurship. His career history includes major jobs at prominent financial institutions, where he sharpened his abilities and insights into the mechanisms of wealth creation.

As an ardent champion of financial literacy, Jordan has committed himself to making the sometimes difficult world of finance accessible to a greater audience. He is a sought-after speaker, having given keynote presentations at renowned financial conferences and led seminars on personal finance and investing techniques.

Beyond his professional pursuits, Jordan is highly devoted to community participation and charity. He actively supports efforts aimed at improving financial education in marginalized areas and argues for the favorable influence of financial well-being on overall life satisfaction.

Jordan's writing reveals not just his skill but also his sincere desire to inspire good change in the lives of his readers. His book, "Pillars of wealth" is a testimony to his comprehensive approach to wealth-building, integrating financial expertise with an emphasis on personal satisfaction.

Table of content

Introduction

Introduction

Setting the Foundation

In a society formed by hopes and ambitions, the chase of riches frequently takes center stage, resonating as a common thread that runs through the fabric of our lives. The idea of wealth goes much beyond the simple acquisition of financial possessions; it embodies a deeper essence, touching upon the desires for a meaningful and secure future.

Wealth, in its purest form, is a multifaceted diamond that incorporates not only monetary riches but also the richness of experiences, possibilities, and a feeling of security. In this trip through the "Pillars of

Wealth," we engage in a quest to understand and appreciate the significant importance of wealth in our lives.

At its root, money is a foundation upon which aspirations are built, offering the means and freedom to pursue a life of purpose and satisfaction. It is the entrance to choices and possibilities, allowing people to create their futures and contribute to the well-being of their communities.

In our quest for prosperity, it is vital to remember that genuine financial well-being exceeds the sheer amassing of cash. A holistic approach is a compass that steers us beyond the limited limitations of monetary achievement, enabling a deliberate investigation of every area of our life.

Holistic financial well-being covers not only financial success but also emotional, mental, and physical well-being. It is a tapestry woven with strands of financial literacy, emotional intelligence, and a profound awareness of personal values and objectives.

In a society typically preoccupied with instant rewards, this holistic approach acts as a lighthouse, reminding us that sustainable wealth is a complicated dance between attentive decision-making, disciplined financial habits, and a keen awareness of the effect of our actions on ourselves and others around us.

As we continue on our trip through the "Pillars of Wealth," we dive into the concept that a wealthy life is one in which financial security coexists peacefully with a sense of purpose, personal satisfaction, and general well-being. This comprehensive strategy helps people not just to amass riches but also to handle life's uncertainties with fortitude and grace.

Together, we will study how each pillar contributes to this larger canvas of well-being, ensuring that our pursuit of money fits perfectly with the drive for a life rich in purpose, connections, and personal development. Let us walk the route to financial well-being with a holistic attitude, realizing that genuine prosperity develops when we balance the different facets of our lives into a symphony of lasting success and satisfaction.

Part I

Building a Strong Financial Foundation

Chapter 1

Financial Literacy

In the complicated tapestry of wealth development, the fundamental pillar upon which our path depends is the thorough grasp of financial literacy. Imagine exploring a wide and dynamic country without a map; similarly, commencing the pursuit of riches without a foundation in financial literacy may lead to confusion and lost opportunities.

Embracing Financial Literacy: A Foundation for Wealth

At its heart, financial literacy is the compass that leads us through the complicated area of personal money. It is not only a collection of data and equations but rather a key to opening the doors of informed decision-making and effective financial management. In this chapter, we dig into the necessity of knowing fundamental financial principles and establish the framework for a path that is both informed and meaningful.

Decoding the Language of Finance

Financial literacy is the bridge that links people with the language of money. Just as one would learn a new language to traverse a distant area, obtaining financial literacy gives us the vocabulary to appreciate the nuances of investments, budgets, and economic trends. By demystifying financial terms, we empower ourselves to make educated decisions and actively engage in our financial path.

Informed Decision-Making for Financial Empowerment

Financial literacy helps people to go beyond passive observers in their financial lives, promoting active involvement and participation. By mastering essential concepts like budgeting, savings, and debt management, people obtain the ability to make educated choices that match their objectives and desires. This information forms the base upon which a sound financial foundation is created, creating resilience in the face of economic adversity.

Navigating the Path to Financial Mastery

Understanding the necessity of financial literacy is simply the beginning of our path toward financial mastery. In this part, we will dig into practical advice and tangible measures that enable people to develop their financial literacy, changing it from a concept into a lived reality.

Embrace continual Learning:

Cultivate an attitude of continual learning by remaining educated about financial trends and changes.
Explore credible resources such as financial periodicals, online courses, and seminars to expand your expertise.

Build a Personal Finance Library:

Create a curated collection of books, articles, and guidelines on personal finance.
Include a range of subjects, from budgeting and investing to retirement planning, to establish a thorough grasp.

Seek Professional Guidance:

Consult with financial advisers or specialists to acquire insights customized to your position.
Attend financial planning workshops or seminars to gain specialized guidance on enhancing your financial strategy.

Utilize Technology:

Leverage financial applications and tools to manage spending, make budgets, and monitor investments.
Stay linked to financial news and updates via appropriate applications, guaranteeing real-time knowledge of market developments.

Engage in Financial Conversations:

Participate in talks with peers, mentors, or financial support groups.

Share experiences and benefit from others' thoughts, getting varied viewpoints on financial concerns.

Practice Budgeting:

Implement a sensible budget that corresponds with your financial objectives. Regularly examine and adapt your budget as circumstances change, developing a habit of financial responsibility.

Gamify Financial Learning:

Explore financial education games and simulations to make learning interesting. Gamification may boost recall and comprehension of financial topics dynamically and engagingly.

Stay Mindful of Your Financial Objectives:

Establish short-term and long-term financial objectives.

Regularly evaluate and reassess these objectives, ensuring that your financial actions fit with your desires.

As we begin on this road to enhance financial literacy, let these practical recommendations be your guide. By adopting these tactics into your everyday life, you not only strengthen your comprehension of fundamental financial concepts but also lay the road for a future marked by financial confidence and empowerment.

Chapter 2

Budgeting Mastery

In the vast orchestration of personal finance, the second pillar, "Budgeting Mastery," takes center stage. Budgeting is more than simply a financial tool; it is a compass that directs us toward our financial objectives, giving a blueprint for successful resource allocation and conscious spending. In this chapter, we go on a quest to learn the art of budgeting, recognizing it as a cornerstone of financial stability and wealth.

Crafting Your Financial Symphony

Budgeting is not a constraining activity; rather, it is a liberating discipline that encourages people to take charge of their financial story. Let us examine the ideas and practical processes that define budgeting mastery, presenting a framework for developing budgets that connect effortlessly with your ambitions and financial well-being.

Understanding the Essence of Budgeting:

Budgeting is a dynamic process that goes beyond simply spending monitoring.
It is a proactive method, enabling people to invest resources purposefully and prioritize financial objectives.

Building Blocks of an Effective Budget:

Income Assessment: Begin by fully examining your sources of income.
Expense Categorization: Classify your expenditures, differentiating between necessary and discretionary spending.

Setting Realistic Financial Goals:

Establish short-term and long-term financial targets that match your desires.
Your budget acts as the roadmap for accomplishing these objectives, ensuring every financial action contributes to your overall financial success.

Emergency Fund Integration:

Allocate a percentage of your budget to creating and managing an emergency fund.
This financial safety net offers a buffer against unanticipated events, boosting overall financial resilience.

Savings and Investments Allocation:

Prioritize saving and investing as vital components of your budget.
Designate particular percentages or amounts toward savings accounts, retirement plans, and investment portfolios.

Frequent review and modifications:

Treat your budget as a living document, subject to frequent reviews and modifications.
Adapt your budget to shifting circumstances, guaranteeing its relevance throughout different life phases.

Budgeting mastery is not about constraint but liberation—a tool that allows you to use resources intelligently, supporting financial stability and opening the doors to future possibilities.

Strategies for Managing and Optimizing Personal Finances

Beyond the core knowledge of budgeting, mastering the art entails employing strategic techniques to manage and maximize personal money. Here, we cover fundamental tactics that transcend budgeting from a conventional financial plan to a dynamic instrument for wealth generation.

Prioritize Essentials:

Identify and prioritize necessary costs, including essentials such as housing, utilities, and food.
Allocate a major amount of your budget to these core demands before tackling discretionary expenditures.

Embrace the 50/30/20 Rule:

Allocate 50% of your income to needs, 30% to discretionary expenditure, and 20% to savings and debt repayment.
This rule gives a basic but efficient foundation for balanced financial allocation.

Track and classify Spending:

Regularly track and classify your expenses to acquire insights into your spending trends.
Use budgeting applications or spreadsheets for a detailed perspective of where your money is going.

Automated Savings and Investments:

Automate transfers to your savings and investment accounts.
Setting up automatic payments guarantees consistency and discipline in increasing your financial savings.

Create a "Fun" Budget:

Allocate a percentage of your budget for discretionary spending on leisure and entertainment. - This proactive strategy allows for fun without jeopardizing your financial objectives.

Debt payback Strategy:

Prioritize high-interest loans in your budget for speedier payback.
Implement a debt payback plan that corresponds with your financial objectives and overall budget.

Regularly Review and Adjust Categories:

Conduct monthly evaluations of your budget categories and alter allocations as required.
Flexibility ensures that your budget stays relevant, adapting to changes in income or financial objectives.

Emergency Fund Maintenance:

Regularly contribute to and examine your emergency fund.
Ensure it matches with your present financial status, providing a safety net for unforeseen needs.

Negotiate and Optimize Bills:

Periodically check recurring invoices and negotiate for lower rates or reductions. Optimize your routine spending to maximize savings within your budget.

As we combine these tactics into our budgeting skills, imagine the process as a dynamic dance of money management. By integrating core concepts with strategic methods, we not only manage our money successfully but also maximize our resources to pave the route for ongoing wealth-building and financial well-being.

Chapter 3

Smart Saving Strategies

In the symphony of wealth development, the third pillar, "Smart Saving Strategies," emerges as a harmonic melody, weaving together the strands of discipline, foresight, and financial resilience. Saving, when addressed with thought and plan, becomes the cornerstone of financial security and a bridge to future possibilities. This chapter unveils the subtleties of smart saving, studying numerous strategies and uncovering the long-term advantages that resound throughout the spectrum of personal finance.

Various Saving Methods

Smart saving is not only a financial habit; it is a mentality that equips people to handle the uncertainties of life with confidence. Let us begin on a voyage to study the multiplicity of saving ways and unearth the lasting advantages that reach well beyond the immediate horizon.

Smart saving is beyond the act of laying money away; it encompasses a systematic approach to creating financial reserves. It is a proactive reaction to life's unpredictabilities, offering a safety net for unanticipated events and a basis for future goals.

Exploring Various Saving Methods:

Traditional Savings Accounts:

Provide liquidity and accessibility for short-term financial objectives. Generally provides lower interest rates but serves as a safe location to put emergency savings.

High-Yield Savings Accounts:
Combine accessibility with greater interest rates compared to typical savings accounts. Ideal for emergency money and short-to-medium-term savings.

Certificates of Deposit (CDs):
Offer fixed interest rates for a certain duration. Suitable for consumers with a medium-term savings perspective who desire greater returns than standard savings accounts.

Automated Transfers:
Set up automated transfers from your checking to savings accounts. Cultivates consistency in saving by making it a regular component of your financial habits.

Retirement Accounts (401(k), IRA):
Provide tax benefits for long-term retirement savings. Act as a significant instrument for creating wealth over a lengthy time.

Investment Portfolios:
Diversify savings by investing in stocks, bonds, or mutual funds. Balances risk and possible reward for long-term wealth growth.

Emergency Funds:
Establish and manage a separate fund to meet unforeseen costs. Serves as a financial safety net, reducing the need to dig into long-term resources for unanticipated events.

Long-Term Benefits of Smart Saving:

Financial Security:

Shield against unforeseen costs or interruptions in income.

Wealth building:
Lay the basis for long-term wealth building via persistent saving and investing.

Freedom and Flexibility:
Provide the financial freedom to seek opportunities and negotiate life adjustments.

Beyond the multitude of saving options, two main components stand out in the symphony of wise saving—emergency money and planned savings. These aspects are the crescendo that fortifies financial resilience and enhances the song of long-term wealth building.

Emergency Funds: A Financial Safety Net

Understanding the Purpose:
An emergency fund acts as a designated pool of money to meet unforeseen costs or income interruptions. It works as a financial safety net, defending against the unpredictable twists that life may provide.

How Much is Enough:
Aim for three to six months' worth of living costs in your emergency fund. Adjust according to your circumstances, risk tolerance, and employment stability.

Liquidity and Accessibility:
Keep emergency savings in readily accessible and liquid accounts. Prioritize accounts with fewer withdrawal limitations to provide speedy access during crises.

Regular Review and Replenishment:
Periodically examine and alter the amount of your emergency fund. Replenish any withdrawn monies swiftly to preserve its efficacy.

Planned Savings: Nurturing Future Aspirations

Defining Your Financial Objectives:
Planned funds are intended for particular financial objectives, such as a house purchase, school, or a dream trip. Establish your objectives and invest cash properly within your intended savings framework.

Consistency is Key:
Establish a regular savings regimen for your desired objectives. Regular donations, even if tiny, build over time and contribute considerably to realizing your ambitions.

Aligning Savings with objectives:
Tailor your saving practices to correspond with the timing and type of your financial objectives. For short-term objectives, emphasize liquidity; for long-term aims, consider investment possibilities for possible growth.

Periodic Evaluation of objectives:
Regularly examine your financial objectives and change your budgeted savings appropriately. Life circumstances may vary, and your savings plan should adapt to growing objectives and priorities.

Balancing Emergency cash and Planned Savings:
Strike a balance between keeping a solid emergency reserve and diverting cash towards planned savings. Careful consideration of short-term requirements

and long-term objectives is vital for good financial planning.

Part II

Investing Wisely for Long-Term Growth

Chapter 4

Introduction to Investing

In the broad tapestry of wealth creation, the fourth pillar, "Introduction to Investing," emerges as a vital movement, orchestrating the possibility for long-term development and financial success. As we continue in this chapter, we dig into the underlying concepts that govern the art of investing, unraveling the complexity to equip you with the knowledge essential to manage the changing environment of financial markets.

Decoding the Essentials

Understanding the Purpose of Investing:
At its essence, investment is the deliberate deployment of resources to earn returns over time. It acts as a mechanism for wealth building, helping people to expand their

financial holdings beyond conventional savings.

Risk and Return:

The Yin and Yang of Investing:
Every investment contains an amount of risk, and understanding this risk-return connection is crucial. Higher potential returns sometimes come with more risk, requiring a judicious balancing depending on individual risk tolerance and financial objectives.

Investment Vehicles:

A Diverse Landscape:
Stocks: Represent ownership in a corporation and give opportunity for financial appreciation and dividends.
Bonds: Debt instruments where investors lend money to entities in exchange for periodic interest payments and repayment of principle.

Mutual Funds: Pools of money from several investors invested in a diverse portfolio of stocks, bonds, or other assets.

Exchange-Traded Funds (ETFs): Similar to mutual funds but traded on stock markets, offering diversity and flexibility.

Time Horizon and Goals:

The length of time you expect to keep an investment, known as the time horizon, determines your investing approach. Align your investing selections with particular financial goals, including short-term and long-term objectives.

Diversification: Spreading the Wealth:

Diversifying your investing portfolio across multiple asset groups minimizes risk. A well-diversified portfolio comprises a mix of stocks, bonds, and maybe other investment products.

Market Basics: Bulls, Bears, and Beyond:

Bull Market: Periods of increasing stock prices, signifying optimism and investor confidence. Bear Market: Periods of dropping stock values, frequently connected with economic downturns. - Understanding market cycles is vital for educated decision-making.

Investment Research and Due Diligence: Thoroughly study possible investments, evaluating financial statements, market trends, and potential hazards. Informed decision-making is the cornerstone of successful investment.

Different Investment Vehicles

In the enormous expanse of investing alternatives, comprehending various vehicles is analogous to picking the correct instruments for a symphony. Let's investigate several investment vehicles, each with its distinctive qualities and possible contributions to your financial composition.

Stocks: Owning a Piece of the Action

Ownership: When you invest in stocks, you become a partial owner of the firm.

Return Potential: Stocks provide the opportunity for financial growth as the firm expands, and some give dividends.

Bonds: A Debt Relationship

Lending Money: Bondholders lend money to governments or businesses in exchange for periodic interest payments and the repayment of principal.

Income Focus: Bonds are generally chosen for dependable income generating.

Mutual Funds: Collective Investing

Diversification: Mutual funds aggregate money from different participants to invest in a diverse portfolio of stocks, bonds, or other assets.

Professional Management: Fund managers make investment choices on behalf of investors.

Exchange-Traded Funds (ETFs): Trading Diversity

Similar to Mutual Funds: ETFs similarly aggregate money from investors but are traded on stock markets like individual equities.

Diversity and Flexibility: ETFs provide diversity and may be purchased or sold during the trading day.

Real Estate Investment Trusts (REITs): Real Estate in Your Portfolio

Real Estate Exposure: REITs are corporations that own, operate or finance income-producing real estate.

Dividends and Capital Appreciation: Investors in REITs may get dividends and profit from capital appreciation.

Index Funds: Mirroring Market Performance

Passive Investment: Index funds try to mirror the performance of a certain market index.
Low Costs: Typically have lower fees compared to actively managed funds.

Certificates of Deposit (CDs): Fixed-Term Savings

Set Term: CDs have a set term and pay interest throughout that time.
Safety: Considered low-risk, making them suited for cautious investors.

Cryptocurrencies: The Digital Frontier

Digital Assets: Cryptocurrencies like Bitcoin run on blockchain technology.

Volatility: Cryptocurrency prices may be very volatile, bringing both dangers and possibilities.

Commodities: Tangible Assets

Physical Goods: Commodities include actual goods like gold, silver, or agricultural products.

Diversity: Investing in commodities may bring diversity to a portfolio.

Understanding the features and functions of these varied investment vehicles helps you to create a well-balanced and harmonious investment portfolio.

Chapter 5

Diversification and Risk Management

In the delicate symphony of investing, the fifth pillar, "Diversification and Risk Management," takes center stage, leading to a beautiful balance of stability and development. This chapter unravels the value of a diverse investment portfolio as a key approach to managing the dynamic and often surprising swings of financial markets.

Harmony in Diversity

Understanding Diversification:

Diversification includes distributing assets over diverse asset classes, sectors, and geographic regions. The idea is to lessen the effect of poor-performing assets on the entire portfolio.

Risk Mitigation Through Diversification:

Different asset classes have diverse risk profiles and react differently to market situations. By having a mix of assets, the total risk of the portfolio may be decreased.

Key Components of a Diversified Portfolio:

Asset Classes:
Stocks: Represent ownership in firms and provide development possibilities.
Bonds: Provide income via interest payments and are typically regarded as less volatile than equities.
Cash or Cash Equivalents: Offer liquidity and stability.

Areas and Industries:
Diversify across areas such as technology, healthcare, finance, and others. This lessens the effect of bad performance in a particular industry on the overall portfolio.

Geographic areas:
Invest in multiple areas or nations to limit exposure to regional economic hazards. Global diversity may offer access to different development prospects.

Investment types:
Consider integrating multiple investment types, such as growth and value investing. This accommodates diverse market situations and investor preferences.

Benefits of a Diversified Portfolio:

- Risk Reduction: Spread risks across several assets, decreasing the effect of a poor-performing investment.

- Smoother Performance: Diversification may contribute to more steady and consistent portfolio performance over time. Market swings in one asset class may be compensated by positive developments in another.

- Increased options: Exposure to diverse asset classes opens the door to a greater variety of investing options. Diversification enables investors to engage in diverse parts of the market.

- Preservation of Capital: Protect capital by reducing the effect of significant reductions in any particular investment. Preservation of capital is vital for long-term financial success.

- Adaptation to Market Changes: A diversified portfolio can respond to changes in economic and market conditions. This flexibility is vital for long-term success in an ever-evolving financial environment.

Beyond recognizing the significance of diversification, competent risk management is the conductor that takes an investor through the dynamic passages of the financial symphony. This section covers concrete techniques to manage and minimize risks within a diversified investment portfolio.

Asset Allocation: A Balancing Act

Strategic Allocation: Determine the appropriate mix of assets depending on your risk tolerance, financial objectives, and time horizon.

Rebalancing: Regularly examine and change your asset allocation to maintain the appropriate balance.

Risk Tolerance Assessment: Know Your Limits

Understand Personal Risk Tolerance: Assess how comfortable you are with various degrees of risk.

Align Investments with Tolerance: Invest in assets that fit your risk appetite, preventing excessive stress during market changes.

Dollar-Cost Averaging: Consistency Amid Volatility

Regular Contributions: Invest a predetermined amount at regular times, regardless of market circumstances.

Potential Benefits: Dollar-cost averaging lessens the effect of market volatility and enables more shares to be acquired during market downturns.

Hedging Strategies: Protection Against Downside Risks

Options Trading: Use options contracts to hedge against future losses in a portfolio.

Insurance products: Consider insurance or other hedging products to protect against certain risks.

Research and Due Diligence: Informed Decision-Making

Thorough Analysis: Conduct exhaustive research before making investing selections.

Stay Informed: Regularly refresh your understanding of market trends, economic data, and possible hazards.

Liquidity Management: Ensuring Accessibility

Maintain Liquid Assets: Ensure a percentage of your portfolio stays in liquid assets.

Emergency Liquidity: Have accessible money for unanticipated financial demands.

Diversification Across Asset Classes: Broadening the Spectrum

Beyond Stocks and Bonds: Explore other assets such as real estate, commodities, or cryptocurrency.

Reducing Correlation: Incorporate assets with low correlation to conventional markets for enhanced diversification.

Stay Disciplined During Market Swings: Emotional Resilience

Long-Term Perspective: Keep a long-term outlook, avoiding hasty actions during short-term market volatility.

Stick to Your Plan: Adhere to your investing plan and prevent making emotional judgments based on market emotions.

Regular Portfolio Reviews: Adaptive Strategy

Periodic Evaluation: Review your portfolio at regular intervals to verify it corresponds with your financial objectives.

Adjustment as Needed: Make modifications depending on changes in your risk tolerance, market circumstances, or financial goals.

By employing these techniques, investors may actively manage and limit risks within their diverse portfolios. Think of these methods as the numerous instruments that contribute to the delicate harmony of your financial composition, giving both stability and resilience as you negotiate the ever-changing world of investing.

Chapter 6

Real Estate and Wealth

In the delicate orchestration of wealth creation, the sixth pillar, "Real Estate and Wealth," emerges as a strong movement, resonating with the ability to construct durable financial foundations. This chapter dives into the essential function of real estate in wealth growth, exposing the specific traits that make it a cornerstone of financial success.

Unveiling the Wealth-Building Power of Real Estate

Real estate offers not simply shelter but a dynamic asset class with the potential for long-term wealth generation. Investment in real estate comprises the strategic purchase, ownership, and administration of physical assets.

Key Aspects of Real Estate Wealth Accumulation:

1. Appreciation: The Growth Engine

Real estate can increase over time, contributing to wealth growth. Properties in favorable areas frequently have greater appreciation rates.

2. Rental Income: A Steady Stream

Owning rental properties offers a continuous source of rental revenue. Rental income offers a layer of diversity to an investment portfolio.

3. Leverage: Amplifying Returns

Investors may utilize borrowed cash to acquire homes, leveraging their investment. Leverage provides for an amplified influence on returns, particularly in appreciating markets.

4. Tax Advantages: Building Wealth Smartly

Deducting mortgage interest may result in considerable tax savings. Real estate investors may benefit from depreciation deductions, decreasing taxable income.

5. Portfolio Diversification: Balancing Risk

Real estate generally demonstrates little correlation with conventional financial assets. Including real estate in a diverse portfolio helps lower overall investment risk.

6. Tangible Asset: A Physical Foundation

Real estate gives physical ownership, creating a feeling of security. Real assets, including property, may operate as a hedge against inflation.

Considerations for Successful Real Estate Investing:

Location Matters:
Invest in locations with potential for economic development and rising demand. Understand local market dynamics and trends.

Property Selection:
Evaluate the possible hazards connected with a property. Choose properties with features that correspond with long-term investing aims.

Financial Management:
Plan for property expenditures, including maintenance, property management, and prospective vacancies. Consider financing choices that correspond with your financial objectives.

Residential and Commercial Real Estate Investments

In the broad area of real estate, the terrain is separated into two basic domains: residential and commercial. Each provides diverse chances and concerns for wealth growth, providing distinctive melodies to the symphony of real estate investing.

Residential Real Estate: The Heart of Homes

- Homeownership and Appreciation: Owning a residential property gives a place to call home while possibly rising in value over time. Residential real estate typically corresponds with emotional and lifestyle ambitions.

- Rental Income Potential: Investment properties, such as single-family houses or flats, may provide rental income. Residential rentals may appeal to a diverse renter population, giving flexibility.

- Leveraging Personal Use: Purchasing a multifamily property enables living in one apartment while renting out others. This model harnesses homeownership for personal usage and money production.

Commercial Real Estate: The Pulse of Business Ventures

- Money via Leasing: Commercial assets, including office spaces, retail units, and industrial spaces, earn money via leasing agreements. Lease lengths in commercial real estate are often longer than residential leases.

- Diverse Tenant Base: Commercial buildings attract a range of tenants, from small enterprises to major multinationals. Diversification in tenant categories may promote stability in revenue sources.

- Potential for larger Returns: Commercial properties frequently provide larger rental returns compared to residential ones. Strategic location and demand for certain kinds of commercial spaces contribute to future development.

- Property Appreciation: Well-located commercial properties may see appreciation, driven by economic growth and demand for commercial spaces. Strategic investments in rising business areas may offer big benefits.

Considerations for Residential and Commercial Real Estate Investments

Risk and Return Dynamics

Residential: Generally considered lower risk, with consistent but modest returns.
Commercial: more potential rewards but frequently coupled with more risk, particularly during economic downturns.

Financing Strategies

Residential: Typically simpler to finance, with different mortgage alternatives available.
Commercial: Financing may demand greater down payments, and terms might vary depending on property type and region.

Management and Involvement

Residential: Management may be more hands-on, particularly for small-scale properties.
Commercial: May entail more professional management, particularly for bigger buildings or complicated projects.

Market Trends and Economic Factors

Residential: Influenced by housing demand, economic growth, and interest rates.
Commercial: Tied to business cycles, industry trends, and particular market needs.

As you negotiate the different landscapes of residential and commercial real estate investments, imagine each property as a separate note contributing to the harmonic arrangement of your real estate symphony.

Whether establishing a house or nurturing commercial initiatives, real estate investments provide a complex route toward permanent wealth growth.

Part III

Entrepreneurship and Wealth Creation

Chapter 7

Entrepreneurial Mindset

In the symphony of wealth creation, the seventh pillar, the "Entrepreneurial Mindset," emerges as a vibrant song, mirroring the inventive energy and resilience that pushes people toward entrepreneurial success. This chapter digs into the attitudes and attributes that distinguish successful entrepreneurs, unraveling the threads of vision, flexibility, and perseverance that constitute the fabric of entrepreneurial activities.

Unveiling the Essence of the Entrepreneurial Mindset

1. Visionary Thinking:

Successful entrepreneurs possess a clear vision of their objectives and the effect they seek to achieve. They foresee future trends and obstacles, leading their endeavors toward long-term success.

2. Adaptability:
Entrepreneurs thrive in dynamic surroundings, accepting change as a chance for progress. Adaptability helps entrepreneurs to pivot, iterate, and enhance their strategy in response to new conditions.

3. Resilience and Tenacity:
Successful entrepreneurs display unshakable tenacity in the face of failures and hurdles. Each difficulty becomes a learning opportunity, driving their desire to conquer adversity.

4. Risk-Taking:
Entrepreneurs are not opposed to taking chances but do it with careful analysis and strategic preparation. They grasp the

balance between risk and reward, reducing possible drawbacks while increasing possibilities.

5. Creativity and Innovation:
Entrepreneurs address challenges with inventive solutions, frequently questioning traditional thinking. They build a culture of innovation, keeping ahead by bringing new ideas and ways.

6. Customer-Centric Focus:
Successful businesses emphasize knowing their target customer. They build goods or services that target client problem spots, delivering actual value.

7. Networking and Relationship Building:
Entrepreneurs establish strong networks, using connections for mentoring, collaborations, and opportunities. Successful entrepreneurs construct talented teams, understanding the cumulative power of varied abilities.

8. Resourcefulness:
Entrepreneurs specialize in resource management, effectively using available assets. They generally start with low cash, learning to be resourceful and inventive in expanding their companies.

9. Continuous Learning:
Successful entrepreneurs have a desire for information and endeavor to grasp market trends and innovations. They regularly educate themselves, keeping relevant in dynamically shifting markets

Entrepreneurial Approach to Opportunities

As we immerse ourselves in the tapestry of entrepreneurial thought, it becomes a call to action, an encouragement to adopt the attitude that has fuelled the success of creative people. Here, we urge readers not simply to comprehend the entrepreneurial mentality but to actively nurture it and apply it to the possibilities that emerge in their own lives.

Embrace Curiosity and Continuous Learning:

Cultivate a curiosity-driven mentality, constantly striving to comprehend, explore, and learn. Lifelong Learning. View each event as a lesson and commit to ongoing learning, adjusting to the ever-evolving world.

Develop a Clear Vision and Set Goals:

Clearly define your aims and imagine the effect you seek to achieve. Break down your vision into actionable objectives, producing a roadmap for your business path.

Embrace Challenges as Opportunities:

Shift your viewpoint on problems, viewing them as chances for development and learning. Develop the resilience to bounce back from setbacks with newfound resolve.

Cultivate an Innovative Mindset:

Question conventional thinking and seek new solutions to challenges. Encourage innovation among your teams and seek out creative responses to common difficulties.

Network and Build Relationships:

Actively connect with varied persons, developing a network that gives support and opportunities. Form partnerships that allow for shared insights, collective progress, and mutual success.

Take Calculated Risks:

Assess risks using a measured manner, recognizing possible benefits and implications. Be willing to venture out of your comfort zone, understanding that progress frequently lies outside familiar regions.

Focus on Value Creation:

Prioritize understanding the requirements of your audience and produce goods or services that bring value. Continuously modify your products depending on client feedback and market needs.

Be Adaptable to Change:

Accept that plans may alter, and be ready to modify tactics depending on shifting conditions. Be open to pivoting as required, seeing change as a chance for creativity.

Encourage a Growth Mindset:

Embrace difficulties as opportunities for personal and professional progress. Treat errors as lessons, enhancing your approach and techniques for future initiatives.

Embrace each opportunity as a chance to create, learn, and establish a legacy of influence. The entrepreneurial mentality is not simply a theory; it is a dynamic force that drives people toward amazing results. Seize the possibilities that come your way, harness your inner entrepreneur, and write your symphony of success.

Chapter 8

Starting and Scaling a Business

In the grand orchestration of entrepreneurship, the eighth pillar, "Starting and Scaling a Business," rises as a crescendo, signifying the transforming journey from concept to business. This chapter is a practical guide, giving specific methods and insights to support budding entrepreneurs as they begin the thrilling journey of founding and expanding their enterprises.

Practical Steps for Starting a Business

Define Your Business Idea:

Identify Your Passion: Start with something you are passionate about or an industry where you see untapped opportunity.

Solve an issue: Address a particular issue or need in the market with your product or service.

Conduct Market Research:

Understand Your Audience: Research your target audience, their tastes, and the current market environment.

Competitor Analysis: Evaluate rivals to find gaps in the market or opportunities for differentiation.

Develop a Comprehensive Business Plan:

Executive Summary: Clearly define your company concept, aims, and purpose.

Market Strategy: Outline your target market, positioning, and marketing strategy.

Financial Projections: Provide accurate financial predictions and projections.

Legal Structure and Registration:

Choose a Legal form: Decide on the legal form of your company (sole proprietorship, LLC, corporation, etc.).
Register Your Business: Complete all essential legal registrations and receive any relevant licenses or permissions.

Secure Funding:

Personal resources: Consider utilizing personal resources for early financing.
Seek Investors or Loans: Explore possibilities like investors, small business loans, or crowdsourcing sites.

Build a Strong Online Presence:

Website Development: Create a professional and user-friendly website to exhibit your goods or services.
Social Media Presence: Utilize social media channels to engage with your audience and develop brand recognition.

Establish Branding and Marketing:

Brand Identity: Develop a strong brand identity, including a recognizable logo and consistent visual components.
Marketing plan: Implement a thorough marketing plan to reach and engage your target audience.

Set Up Financial Management Systems:

Accounting Software: Choose dependable accounting software to monitor revenue, spending, and financial transactions.
Financial rules: Establish clear financial rules and processes for your firm.

Hire and Build a Team:

Identify important responsibilities: Determine the important responsibilities required to manage your company efficiently.

Recruitment: Hire people with the talents and enthusiasm to contribute to your business's success.

Implement Scalable Systems:

Scalable procedures: Design operational procedures that can expand as your firm develops.

Technology Integration: Leverage technology to automate repetitive processes and simplify operations.

Focus on Customer Service:

Customer-Centric Approach: Prioritize great customer service to develop trust and loyalty.

Input Mechanisms: Establish avenues for consumer input to constantly enhance your products.

Adapt and Iterate:

Stay Agile: Embrace an agile attitude, be open to criticism, and adjust your strategy depending on market conditions.
Continuous Improvement: Implement a culture of continuous improvement, iterating on both goods and processes.

Strategies for Scaling a Business for Sustained Growth

As the entrepreneurial journey develops, the symphony changes from the early chords of invention to the harmonies of growth and scalability. This section digs into crucial tactics that entrepreneurs may utilize to scale their firms for sustainable development, ensuring that the melody of success resonates beyond greater horizons.

Strategic Planning for Growth:

Define explicit, quantifiable, and realistic objectives for company development. Align short-term initiatives with a long-term vision for sustainable development.

Market Expansion and Diversification:

Identify and appraise the potential for growth into new geographic areas. Consider broadening your product or service offerings to target a larger client base.

Technology Integration and Automation:

Embrace innovative technology to simplify procedures and boost operational efficiency. Automate repetitive processes to free up resources for strategic objectives.

Scalable Infrastructure:

Implement scalable systems and infrastructure capable of handling rising demand. Leverage cloud-based solutions for flexibility and scalability.

Build Strategic Partnerships:

Form strategic alliances that mutually benefit both firms. Tap into existing networks for possible partnerships and synergies.

Talent Acquisition and Development:

Recruit personnel with talents that correspond with your growth plan. Invest in training and development programs to strengthen the skills of your workforce.

Customer Retention and Expansion:

Implement loyalty programs to retain current consumers. Explore chances to upsell or cross-sell additional items or services to current clients.

Financial Management and Funding:

Maintain a comprehensive financial management system, with clear budgeting for growth projects. Explore new financing sources to support growth ambitions.

Streamlined Operations:

Continuously review and improve operational procedures for enhanced efficiency. Streamline supply chain procedures to save costs and boost responsiveness.

Monitor Key Performance Indicators (KPIs):

Use KPIs to monitor and assess company performance. Iterative plans: Adjust plans depending on real-time data and market reaction.

Brand Building and Marketing Expansion:

Strengthen your brand with consistent messaging and exceptional offers. Explore new marketing channels to reach a bigger audience.

Regulatory Compliance and Risk Management:

Ensure compliance with appropriate rules in new markets or sectors. Implement techniques to identify and reduce possible risks connected with expansion.

As you expand your company, see these techniques as the dynamic notes that contribute to the crescendo of sustainable growth. The entrepreneurial symphony continues to develop, and with strategic planning, adaptation, and a focus on scalability, you may compose a story of ongoing success and growth in the commercial environment.

Part IV

Mindset and Lifestyle

Chapter 9

Mindset Matters

In the complex symphony of wealth creation, the ninth pillar, "Mindset Matters," takes center stage, resonating with the subtle but deep psychological notes that form the road toward affluence. This chapter dives into the psychological components of wealth development, revealing the mentality adjustments and mental frameworks that play a key part in the quest for financial success.

Psychological Aspects of Wealth Creation

Positive Thinking and Abundance Mindset:

The Power of Positivity: Cultivate an optimistic view on wealth creation, believing in the possibilities that lay ahead.
Abundance Mentality: Embrace an abundance mentality, viewing possibilities as numerous rather than scarce.

Goal Setting and Visualization:

Clarity in Objectives: Set clear and defined financial objectives, giving a blueprint for your wealth journey.
Visualization Techniques: Use visualization to mentally visualize your objectives, improving motivation and attention.

Overcoming Limiting Beliefs:

Identify and confront Limitations: Acknowledge and confront self-limiting ideas that may inhibit financial achievement.

Cultivate Self-Empowerment: Replace limiting ideas with powerful thoughts and affirmations.

Risk-Taking and Resilience:

Embrace calculated risks: Develop a healthy relationship with risk, realizing that it is important to wealth generation.
Resilience in Setbacks: Cultivate resilience to bounce back from financial setbacks, seeing them as learning opportunities.

Delayed Gratification and Patience:

Deferred Rewards: Practice delayed gratification, forsaking short-term pleasures for long-term financial rewards.
Patience as a Virtue: Understand that wealth generation is a gradual process, requiring patience and tenacity.

Financial Literacy and Continuous Learning:

Empowerment via Knowledge: Develop a firm foundation in financial literacy, helping you to make educated choices.
Lifelong Learning: Cultivate an attitude of continual learning, remaining updated about altering financial environments.

Adapting to Change:

Flexibility in Thinking: Embrace adaptation, realizing that financial markets and opportunities are dynamic.
Learning from errors: View changes and errors as important learning experiences, adapting strategy appropriately.

Generosity and Abundance Sharing:

Generosity as a Catalyst: Cultivate a giving attitude, realizing that donating to others may bring abundance.

Philanthropy and influence: Consider how your wealth creation may favorably influence not just your life but the lives of others.

Emotional Intelligence in Financial Decision-Making:

Awareness of Emotions: Develop emotional intelligence to understand and regulate your emotions in financial decision-making.
Balancing Rationality and Emotion: Find a balance between logical analysis and emotional awareness to make healthy financial decisions.

Gratitude and Contentment:

Appreciation Practice: Cultivate a practice of appreciation, recognizing the resources and opportunities in your life.
Contentment Amid Ambition: Balance ambition with contentment, finding

pleasure in the journey while working for financial objectives.

The Impact of a Positive Mindset on Financial Success

In the delicate dance between thought and behavior, the influence of a good mentality on financial success is transformational. This section looks into the significant ways in which establishing a good mental framework impacts the trajectory of wealth creation and produces a harmonic confluence of goal and achievement.

Enhanced Problem-Solving Skills:

An optimistic outlook boosts problem-solving abilities, allowing people to tackle obstacles with ingenuity and resilience. Positivity encourages resourcefulness, boosting the capacity to discover inventive solutions to financial challenges.

Attraction of Opportunities:

The belief in the law of attraction claims that good thoughts attract favorable consequences. A positive mentality cultivates awareness, making people more competent at seeing and grasping possibilities for financial gain.

Increased Resilience in Setbacks:

Positivity causes a change in perspective, helping people to perceive setbacks as transient and surmountable. Resilience in the face of adversities converts setbacks into important learning experiences, moving people forward.

Improved Decision-Making:

A positive mentality increases clarity in decision-making, lessening the effect of emotional biases. Individuals with an optimistic view tend to handle risk with a balanced and calculating mentality, making better educated financial choices.

Heightened Motivation and Focus:

Positivity drives intrinsic motivation, promoting a deep-seated desire to attain financial objectives. A positive mentality aids in continuous attention to long-term goals, minimizing distractions and preserving commitment.

Cultivation of Ambitious Goals:

Positive thinkers are more inclined to create ambitious and imaginative financial objectives. A positive mentality instills a strong confidence in one's potential to reach even the loftiest objectives.

Healthy Relationship with Wealth:

Individuals with a positive mentality equate prosperity with satisfaction, stability, and opportunity for personal and social contribution. A positive viewpoint typically goes beyond personal benefit, creating a willingness to utilize riches for altruistic goals.

Enhanced Financial Habits:

A positive mentality adds to disciplined financial behaviors, such as budgeting, saving, and investing. Positive thinkers are more likely to develop and keep practices that lead to sustained wealth growth.

Adaptability to Market Changes:

Positivity promotes adaptation to shifting market circumstances, helping people handle economic volatility with a positive perspective. Rather than dreading change, a positive mentality views it as an outlet for uncovering new chances and paths for financial success.

Impact on Emotional Well-Being:

A positive perspective improves emotional well-being, minimizing stress and anxiety associated with financial problems. The connection between financial success and emotional well-being generates a more comprehensive and durable feeling of accomplishment.

Chapter 10

Balancing Lifestyle and Wealth

Amidst the crescendo of wealth development, the eleventh pillar, "Balancing Lifestyle and Wealth," emerges as a harmonizing refrain, highlighting the necessity of balance in the delicate dance of life and financial success. This chapter looks into the issue of work-life balance, analyzing how the interaction between personal well-being and wealth production adds to a symphony of lasting success and satisfaction.

The Importance of Work-Life Balance

Preserving Physical and Mental Health:

Work-life balance secures both physical and mental health, establishing a basis for sustainable wealth growth. Prioritizing balance helps decrease the danger of burnout, guaranteeing a healthy and resilient response to life's difficulties.

Enhanced Productivity and Creativity:

Time away from work functions as a restorative force, regenerating mental capabilities and boosting overall productivity. A balanced lifestyle provides an atmosphere where creative thoughts develop, leading to inventive solutions in both personal and professional arenas.

Strengthened Relationships:

Balancing business duties with personal life allows for the building of meaningful relationships via quality time spent with family and friends. Strong connections contribute to emotional well-being, establishing a support structure that enhances both personal and financial elements of life.

Mitigation of Stress and Anxiety:

Work-life balance functions as a buffer against stress and anxiety linked with the demands of a high-paced professional life. Individuals with balanced lives are better suited to overcome financial issues with emotional resilience.

Sustainable Financial Success:

Balancing lifestyle and work supports financial success by reducing burnout and preserving a healthy mentality toward wealth growth. A balanced life approach leads to the production of lasting wealth, considering not only financial benefits but overall well-being.

Personal Growth and Development:

Balancing lifestyle supports a commitment to personal improvement beyond professional successes. Allocating time to personal interests and hobbies develops a feeling of contentment and adds to a well-rounded existence.

Alignment with Values and Priorities:

Balancing lifestyle helps people to connect financial choices with their beliefs and objectives. A conscientious approach to wealth building evaluates the influence on lifestyle and ensures financial goals fit with individual beliefs.

Increased Job Satisfaction:

A balanced attitude to work and personal life promotes overall job happiness, generating a positive feedback loop between personal well-being and professional achievement. Job happiness leads to job length, allowing for continuous wealth accumulation over time.

Time for Reflection and Planning:

Work-life balance gives the required time for strategic contemplation on financial objectives and personal ambitions. Individuals with balanced lives are more likely to participate in deliberate financial planning for future milestones and retirement.

Harmonizing Ambition with Enjoyment:

A balanced lifestyle harmonizes ambitious financial objectives with the pleasure of life's events. Riches building is not an isolated quest but a part of a holistic journey where the symphony of life and riches combine.

Strategies for Maintaining a Fulfilling Lifestyle While Building Wealth

As we examine the delicate interaction between lifestyle and money, this part uncovers practical techniques to maintain a harmonic balance, ensuring that the pursuit of financial success improves rather than detracts from the richness of life.

Establish Clear Boundaries:

Set clear limits for work hours to avoid encroachment into personal time. Implement technology detox intervals to withdraw from work-related contacts during personal and family moments.

Prioritize Self-Care:

Incorporate regular exercise into your routine to boost physical and mental well-being. Embrace mindfulness activities such as meditation or yoga to ease stress and boost attention.

Quality Family Time:

Dedicate certain periods for family activities to enhance connections. Establish times without technological gadgets, encouraging meaningful interactions with loved ones.

Set Realistic Financial Goals:

Define financial goals that correspond with your desired lifestyle and beliefs. Acknowledge and appreciate financial accomplishments without compromising personal happiness.

Flexible Work Arrangements:

If practical, seek flexible work options such as remote work or flexible scheduling. Negotiate perks that enhance work-life balance, such as flexible hours or extended time off.

Outsource Non-Core Tasks:

Delegate non-core chores, both at work and home, to free up time for activities that offer pleasure and satisfaction. Concentrate your attention on high-priority projects, optimizing your time for the greatest effect.

Regular Financial Check-Ins:

Set regular intervals for financial reviews, ensuring your wealth-building tactics correspond with your developing lifestyle. Be flexible to adapt financial plans when personal priorities and circumstances change.

Plan and Budget for Experiences:

Allocate cash expressly for experiences and activities that add to your general well-being. Recognize that experiences may be equally important as material items in establishing a meaningful living.

Continuous Communication with Partners:

Maintain open conversation with partners or family members regarding financial objectives and lifestyle preferences. Make financial choices cooperatively, ensuring that everyone's needs and preferences are recognized.

Embrace the Power of No:
Learn to say no to obligations that do not line with your objectives and beliefs. Prioritize personal time and protect against overcommitting to work or social responsibilities.

Invest in Education and Skills:

Allocate time and resources for continual education and skill development. Learning new talents may be both satisfying and contribute to long-term professional progress.

Create a Holistic Vision Board:

Develop a vision board that covers both financial and lifestyle aspirations. Regularly review and revise the vision board to ensure alignment with shifting ambitions.

Balancing lifestyle and money is a continual process that demands conscious decisions, and with strategic integration, you may arrange a symphony where each note adds to a life rich in both monetary and experience riches.

Conclusion

Chapter 11

Reflection on the Pillars

As the symphony of wealth creation reaches its crescendo, this chapter asks you to reflect on the deep trip through the 10 pillars that have lit the way to financial success. Let's extract the essence of each pillar, encapsulating fundamental notions that form the cornerstone of a harmonic and intentional approach to wealth building.

Setting the Foundation

Establish a basic grasp of wealth and its importance. Emphasize that wealth goes beyond monetary worth, embracing well-being, relationships, and personal satisfaction.

Holistic Approach to Financial Well-Being

Highlight the necessity for a complete approach to financial well-being. Emphasize the synergy between financial health, emotional well-being, and personal satisfaction.

Entrepreneurial Mindset

Explore the attitude and qualities of successful entrepreneurs. Encourage readers to build an entrepreneurial attitude to possibilities, boosting creativity and resilience.

Starting and Scaling a Business

Guide people through practical stages for launching a company, from concept inspiration to operational launch. Techniques for growing: Discuss important techniques for growing a firm, guaranteeing sustainable growth and flexibility.

Mindset Matters

Explore the psychological components of wealth creation, diving into the power of positive thinking and overcoming limiting beliefs. Discuss the enormous influence of a positive mentality on financial success, spanning problem-solving, decision-making, and attracting opportunities.

Balancing Lifestyle and Wealth

Reflect on the value of work-life balance in generating lasting prosperity and overall life contentment. Introduce realistic ways for sustaining a satisfying lifestyle while increasing money, stressing the integration of personal and financial objectives.

Encouragement to Reflect on Your Financial Journey

As we negotiate the complicated tapestry of wealth building, it's vital to stop and engage in contemplation. Consider this chapter an opportunity to reflect on your financial path, gaining inspiration from the pillars examined so far.

Acknowledge Your Starting Point:

Consider your first notion of wealth and how it has changed. Acknowledge the progress accomplished in creating a comprehensive foundation for your financial path.

Assess Your Holistic Well-Being:

Reflect on your approach to financial well-being. How balanced is your perspective? Are there places where you can increase the synergy between financial health and general well-being?

Embrace an Entrepreneurial Mindset:

Recognize the entrepreneurial traits you relate with. How have these attributes affected your decision-making and pursuit of opportunities?

Contemplate Your Business Journey:

If you've launched on business project, evaluate the practical actions necessary to start and grow. What methods have helped to development, and how have you reacted to challenges?

Assess Your Mindset:

Reflect on your thinking. Have you established an optimistic mindset, and how has it benefited your financial success?

Identify examples when overcoming limiting beliefs led to favorable results.

Balance Lifestyle and Wealth:

Consider how successfully you've matched lifestyle and wealth-building. Which tactics connect with you, and how have you blended personal and financial goals?

Envision Your Symphony:

Envision your financial path as a symphony. What notes symbolize your triumphs, struggles, and the balanced interplay of lifestyle and wealth?

Set Future Melodies:

Look forward and establish the melody for the future. What financial objectives connect with your beliefs and desired lifestyle? How can you further enhance the melody of your financial journey?

Celebrate Your Progress:

Take a minute to celebrate your financial accomplishments, both large and small. Acknowledge the development you've experienced and the lessons learned along the road.

Embrace Continuous Refinement:

Embrace an attitude of constant progress. How can you optimize your financial plans and boost your general well-being? What lessons from the pillars may influence your future decisions?

This contemplative trip is a vital aspect of the symphony, helping you to construct the following sections in your financial story.

Chapter 12

Creating Your Personal Wealth Plan

As the crescendo of thought settles into a tranquil moment, it's time to grab the reins of your financial path with purpose and intention. In this chapter, we begin the adventure of "Creating Your Personal Wealth Plan," helping you through the process of constructing a unique plan for growing wealth that corresponds with your objectives and beliefs.

Guide to Developing Your Customized Wealth-Building Plan

Clarify Your Financial Goals:

Define Short and Long-Term Objectives: Clearly explain your financial objectives, differentiating between short-term milestones and long-term ambitions.
Connect with Values: Ensure that your objectives connect with your fundamental values and contribute to your overall well-being.

Assess Your Current Financial Situation:

Revenue and spending: Evaluate your present revenue sources and spending to identify your financial baseline.
Debt Analysis: Assess current debts and establish a strategy for managing and lowering them.

Build an Emergency Fund:

Establish Financial Safety Net: Set aside monies for an emergency fund to offer a safety net for unforeseen costs.
Determine Optimal Size: Determine the ideal amount of your emergency fund depending on your lifestyle and financial commitments.

Craft a Budget:

Create a Realistic Budget: Develop a precise budget that allocates monies for basics, discretionary expenditure, and savings.
Routinely review and Adjust: Commit to routinely evaluating and altering your budget to line with changing circumstances and objectives.

Explore Investment Strategies:

Understand Risk Tolerance: Assess your risk tolerance to discover viable investing methods.
Diversify Portfolio: Explore varied investment alternatives to improve long-term returns while minimizing risk.

Save for Specific Goals:

Prioritize Savings: Allocate cash toward particular objectives such as housing, school, or travel.
Tailor Saving Techniques: Customize your saving techniques depending on the schedule and size of each objective.

Consider Retirement Planning:

Evaluate Retirement requirements: Estimate your retirement requirements and design a strategy to secure financial stability throughout retirement.

Explore Retirement Accounts: Explore numerous retirement accounts and investment options to improve your retirement funds.

Optimize Tax Planning:

Understand Tax consequences: Gain complete awareness of tax consequences relating to your income, investments, and financial choices.

Leverage Tax-Advantaged Accounts: Explore possibilities to maximize tax advantages via strategic usage of tax-advantaged accounts.

Review and Adjust Periodically:

Schedule Regular Reviews: Establish a system for evaluating and updating your wealth strategy regularly.

Accommodate Life Changes: Be prepared to alter your strategy to suit big life changes, such as professional transfers, family relationships, or economic challenges.

Educate Yourself Continuously:

Commit to Lifelong Learning: Stay educated about financial trends, investment strategies, and personal finance best practices.
Seek Professional Advice: Consider engaging financial experts for experienced help and insights.

Actionable Steps Based on the Pillars

As you dig into the design of your wealth strategy, let the major principles from the pillars act as guiding lights. Here are concrete methods inspired by the pillars to infuse your strategy with meaning and actionable intent:

Set Your Vision

Clearly outline your vision for prosperity. Envision not only financial success, but a life full of adventures, relationships, and personal pleasure.

Adopt a Holistic Approach

Assess your money strategy from a comprehensive approach. Ensure that it incorporates not just financial considerations but also your emotional well-being, relationships, and general life happiness.

Embrace an Entrepreneurial Mindset

Infuse your wealth strategy with an entrepreneurial attitude. Identify chances for innovation, creativity, and flexibility in your financial pursuits.

Take Practical Steps

Translate your objectives into real actions. If entrepreneurship is part of your goal, identify clear measures for launching and expanding your business.

Cultivate a Positive Mindset

Foster a positive mentality in your wealth plan. Set objectives, employ affirmations, and picture success to alter your mindset and decision-making.

Balance Lifestyle and Wealth

Prioritize work-life balance in your strategy. Identify precise tactics to combine personal and financial objectives, guaranteeing a harmonic and enjoyable path.

Reflect on Your Journey

Build introspective times into your wealth strategy. Regularly examine your progress, appreciate triumphs, and modify the course depending on life's lessons.

Customize Your Strategies

Tailor your wealth-building techniques to match with your objectives, values, and circumstances. Avoid a one-size-fits-all approach and embrace the individualized aspect of your strategy.

By following these concrete activities inspired by the pillars, your wealth strategy changes from a theoretical framework into a living roadmap. Infuse it with your energy, alter it as required, and allow it to lead you toward a life where financial achievement is not simply a goal but an intrinsic part of a symphony of satisfaction and prosperity.

Chapter 13

Empowering Future Generations

In the symphony of wealth building, the thirteenth chapter, "Empowering Future Generations," encourages you to ponder the permanent influence of your financial journey. This chapter offers a guide to ways to pass on financial knowledge to the next generation, ensuring that the symphony of success echoes beyond your lifetime.

Strategies for Passing on Wealth Knowledge to the Next Generation

Cultivate Financial Literacy:

Start the road early by teaching fundamental financial ideas to youngsters.

Engage in talks about money concerns, including children in age-appropriate discussions about budgeting, saving, and investing.

Lead by Example:

Demonstrate good financial habits via your actions and choices. Narrate personal experiences and success stories, offering practical insights into wealth building.

Establish Family Values:

Identify family values relating to money, generosity, and financial responsibility. Demonstrate how these values shape financial choices and priorities.

Create Financial Goals Together:

Conduct family talks to create collective financial objectives. Encourage each family member to contribute their thoughts and ambitions to the joint financial plan.

Teach Responsible Spending:

Involve younger family members in age-appropriate budgeting activities. Foster an awareness of responsible spending by examining the difference between needs and desires.

Introduce the Concept of Investing:

Facilitate a hands-on experience by introducing simulated investment for educational reasons. Discuss the notion of risk and reward in investing, stressing the need for educated decision-making.

Plan for Inheritance:

Have open and upfront talks regarding inheritance planning. Emphasize the obligations involved with inherited money, including stewardship and the potential for impact.

Engage in Philanthropy Together:

Collaborate on charitable efforts as a family, developing a feeling of social responsibility. Visit charity organizations together to observe the effect of giving firsthand.

Utilize Technology for Education:

Leverage educational applications and Internet tools to make financial learning entertaining and interactive. Explore digital platforms that provide financial simulations for practical learning experiences.

Foster Entrepreneurial Spirit:

Nurture creativity and innovation by creating an entrepreneurial mentality. Provide direction and support for family members pursuing their business dreams.

Create a Family Wealth Mission Statement

Develop a family wealth mission statement collectively, expressing shared values and objectives. Treat the mission statement as a live document that changes with the family's objectives and circumstances.

Legacy Mindset:

Beyond the transmission of financial information, creating a legacy attitude is a significant feature of empowering future generations. Here are some techniques to establish a legacy attitude among your family:

Articulate the Importance of Legacy:

Family talks: Initiate open talks about the importance of legacy and the influence it may have on future generations.

Historical Narratives: Share family tales and histories that stress the ongoing character of legacies.

Emphasize Values Over Material Wealth:

Values-Centric talks: Prioritize talks around family values above discussions exclusively focused on monetary prosperity.

Integrity and Ethics: Stress the significance of ethical conduct and integrity as vital components of the family heritage.

Encourage Intergenerational Conversations:

Generational Dialogues: Facilitate talks between various generations within the family.

Shared Experiences: Encourage the sharing of experiences, ideas, and lessons learned across generations.

Document Family Stories and Wisdom:

Family Archives: Create a storehouse for family memories, knowledge, and experiences.
Collaborative Documentation: Involve family members in the process of recording tales to develop a collaborative legacy archive.

Establish Family Traditions:

Legacy-Building Traditions: Introduce traditions that stress the handing down of values, tales, and distinctive family rituals.
Symbolic Rituals: Develop rituals that signify the continuity of the family lineage.

Mentorship Across Generations:

Formal Mentorship Programs: Establish mentorship programs inside the family, matching experienced members with younger ones.

Skill and Knowledge transmission: Encourage the transmission of skills, knowledge, and expertise as part of the mentoring process.

Invest in Education and Learning:

Legacy Scholarships: Institute scholarships or educational funds with an emphasis on continuing a legacy of learning.

Encourage Lifelong Learning: Emphasize the need for continued education and personal growth as vital to the family heritage.

Stewardship of Family Assets:

Educate on Stewardship: Teach the ideas of responsible stewardship for family assets, stressing the obligation to protect and build wealth for future generations.

Integrate charity: Incorporate charity into the stewardship narrative, stressing the beneficial influence the family can have on society.

Involve Younger Generations in Decision-Making:

Participatory Decision-Making: Include younger family members in important decision-making processes.
Teach Responsible Decision-Making: Provide direction on making responsible choices that accord with the family's heritage and beliefs.

Encourage Individual Contributions to the Legacy:

Distinctive Contributions: Acknowledge and promote each family member's distinctive contributions to the family heritage.

Expressive channels: Provide creative channels for expressing individual viewpoints on the family's heritage, such as painting, writing, or storytelling.

Encouraging a legacy attitude is a transformational activity that spans generations. By cultivating a profound feeling of connection to family values and a dedication to the well-being of future generations, you contribute to a legacy that reaches well beyond financial prosperity, producing a lasting influence on the identity and purpose of your family.

Chapter 14

Beyond Wealth: Fulfillment and Contribution

In the dramatic conclusion of our riches symphony, Chapter 14 urges you to surpass the customary limitations of affluence. Titled "Beyond Wealth: Fulfillment and Contribution," this chapter discusses the tremendous influence of riches on personal contentment and the transformational potential of contributing to a higher cause.

Exploring the Broader Impact of Wealth on Personal Fulfillment

Wealth as a Catalyst for Personal Growth:

Wealth, when addressed with purpose, becomes a catalyst for various and rewarding life experiences. Personal development thrives when affluence affords possibilities for ongoing learning and self-discovery.

Meaningful Connections and Relationships:

Beyond financial rewards, money may cultivate excellent relationships and meaningful connections. Shared experiences develop ties, leading to a gratifying and rich tapestry of social connections.

The Intersection of Passion and Purpose:

Wealth affords the flexibility to follow hobbies and interests that correspond with personal ideals. When money aligns with purpose, it becomes a vehicle for contributing to causes greater than oneself.

Impactful Philanthropy:

Consider the transformational potential of money in supporting effective philanthropic projects. We study how focused donations may achieve quantifiable change and have a lasting beneficial influence on communities.

Legacy of Contribution:

Wealth, when utilized to contribute to society, is the cornerstone of a meaningful and contributive legacy. Beyond monetary inheritance, we dive into the legacy of values and contributions handed on to future generations.

Holistic Well-Being:

Wealth, when incorporated into a balanced life strategy, adds to overall well-being. We study how human satisfaction transcends financial achievement, including physical, mental, and emotional well-being.

The Joy of Giving:

Explore the emotional benefits received from the act of giving, understanding the pleasure and fulfillment that philanthropy may provide. Wealth becomes a tool for developing a greater connection to the community and contributing to its wellbeing.

Entrepreneurial Contributions:

Wealth created via entrepreneurial businesses may fuel innovation and have a greater social influence. We study how entrepreneurs might use their resources to achieve good change, both inside and beyond their businesses.

Reflection on Personal Values:

Encouraging meditation on aligning wealth development with personal values, highlighting that satisfaction derives from a values-driven approach. Delve into the necessity of thoughtful decision-making in wealth-related concerns to guarantee alignment with fundamental values.

Sustainable Contributions:

Investigate how money might be utilized to create sustainable contributions, addressing environmental and social concerns. Examine the potential for riches to leave a good and lasting impact via sustainable activities.

Opportunities for Contributing to Society and Making a Positive Impact

In the quest for personal satisfaction and service, this section explores numerous paths through which money may be a catalyst for good change in society:

Philanthropic Endeavors:

Establishing Foundations: Delve into the development of charitable foundations as an organized mechanism to donate to humanitarian concerns.

Focused Giving: Explore the effect of focused giving, concentrating on particular locations or communities that correspond with personal beliefs.

Supporting Education Initiatives:

Scholarship Programs: Discuss the transformational potential of sponsoring scholarship programs, giving access to education for persons who would not have had the chance.

Educational Infrastructure: Explore contributions to the advancement of educational infrastructure, encouraging learning settings for generations to come.

Health and Wellness Initiatives:

Medical Research supporting: Investigate the role of wealth in supporting medical research to accelerate discoveries and enhance global health outcomes.

Community Health Programs: Explore the benefits of supporting community health programs, especially in marginalized communities.

Environmental Sustainability:

Investing in Sustainable Activities: Discuss the role of money in supporting and investing in environmentally sustainable activities, contributing to the battle against climate change.

Conservation initiatives: Explore options for contributing to conservation initiatives, conserving biodiversity and natural resources.

Social Entrepreneurship Ventures:

Investing in Social Enterprises: Explore the notion of social entrepreneurship and how money may be funneled into initiatives that solve social or environmental concerns.

Balancing Profit and Purpose: Discuss models where financial success and positive effect coexist, highlighting the potential for enterprises to be a force for good.

Community Development Projects:

Infrastructure Investments: Examine the effect of investing in community development initiatives, such as infrastructure, housing, and local businesses.

Empowering Local Economies: Discuss how wealth may empower local economies, supporting sustainable development and boosting overall living standards.

Crisis Response and Humanitarian Aid:

Quick Response efforts: Explore the role of wealth in sponsoring quick response efforts during emergencies, offering urgent relief to impacted people.

Long-Term Recovery: Discuss the possibility of continuous assistance to help with long-term recovery efforts after natural disasters or humanitarian crises.

Art and Culture Preservation:

Endowing Cultural Institutions: Explore how money may be utilized to endow cultural institutions, assuring the preservation and promotion of art, literature, and history.

Helping Creativity: Discuss prospects for helping budding artists and innovators, contribute to the richness of cultural landscapes.

Microfinance and Economic Empowerment:

Investing in Microfinance: Delve into the effect of investing in microfinance as a strategy for economic empowerment, especially in emerging nations.

Entrepreneurial assist: Explore methods in which money might be utilized to assist entrepreneurship, generating chances for people to develop sustainable enterprises.

Advocacy for Social Change:

Sponsoring Advocacy Organizations: Discuss the role of wealth in sponsoring advocacy organizations and movements that aim for constructive social change.

Influencing Policy: Explore options for leveraging wealth as a tool to influence policy reforms that address systemic challenges.

As you contemplate these options for contributing to society, let them serve as motivation to build a legacy of influence. Whether via focused charity, sustainable investments, or advocacy for good change, the influence of your money may transcend generations, leaving a lasting impression on the globe.

Final Thoughts

Chapter 15

Final Thoughts on Sustainable Wealth

As we come to the completion of our trip, "Final Thoughts on Sustainable Wealth" serves as a contemplative time to underline the comprehensive aspect of establishing lasting success. This chapter reiterates that genuine riches are not only financial; it is a harmonic symphony that echoes across every part of life.

Reiterating the Holistic Nature of Building Sustainable Wealth

Wealth Beyond Finances:

Comprehensive Well-Being: Sustainable wealth goes beyond financial success, embracing physical, emotional, and mental well-being.

Richness in Relationships: Recognize the richness that meaningful relationships and connections give to the complete tapestry of riches.

Holistic Approach to Finance:

Balanced Financial Health: Emphasize the significance of maintaining a balanced financial strategy that incorporates short-term aims, long-term ambitions, and the ever-changing panorama of life.

Adaptable Financial plans: Advocate for adaptable financial plans that develop with personal circumstances and the larger economic environment.

Entrepreneurial Spirit:

Innovation and Resilience: Acknowledge the entrepreneurial spirit as a driving factor behind sustainable prosperity. Innovation and resilience are crucial components of an enduring financial legacy.

Ethical Business Practices: Highlight the value of ethical business practices, highlighting that genuine prosperity is generated with integrity and a dedication to social well-being.

Contributions to Society:

Impactful Philanthropy: Reinforce the concept that sustainable wealth is interwoven with meaningful contributions to society. Philanthropy becomes a vehicle for riches to achieve beneficial and sustainable change.

Legacy of Values: Explore how passing on values and a commitment to social well-being forms a vital aspect of a sustainable legacy.

Continuous Growth and Learning:

Lifelong Learning: Advocate for the necessity of ongoing development and learning in the quest for sustainable prosperity. An attitude of inquiry and adaptation promotes continuing personal and financial progress.

Flexibility: Emphasize the role of flexibility, both in personal growth and financial strategies, as a vital part of sustainability.

Balance Between Lifestyle and Financial Goals:

Harmonizing Lifestyle and Finances: Reiterate the idea of balance, stressing the need to harmonize lifestyle ambitions with financial goals.

Fulfilling Lives: Sustainable prosperity is not about acquiring money for their own sake but about supporting satisfying lifestyles that match with one's beliefs and objectives.

Legacy as a Living Story:

Dynamic Legacy Building: Encourage the concept of legacy as a living, dynamic tale that is written by deliberate acts, values, and contributions.

Generational influence: Consider the lasting influence of a well-constructed legacy on future generations, indicating that the tale of wealth stretches well beyond the person.

Environmental and Social Responsibility:

Stewardship of Resources: Promote the stewardship of resources, both financial and environmental, as a duty that comes with sustainable affluence.

Beneficial Impact: Acknowledge the potential for money to be a beneficial factor in tackling environmental concerns and contributing to social development.

Reflection and Mindful Decision-Making:

Contemplative Wealth building: Encourage contemplative techniques and attentive decision-making in wealth building. Sustainable wealth develops from conscious decisions connected with personal ideals.

Integrity in judgments: Remind that judgments made with integrity and a sense of purpose contribute to the ongoing sustainability of wealth.

The Symphony of Sustainable Wealth:

The Ever-Evolving Symphony: Conclude with the metaphor of a symphony, showing sustainable prosperity as an ever-evolving composition that resonates with satisfaction, contribution, and a meaningful legacy.

Embark on Their Journey with Confidence and Purpose:

As you stand at the doorway of your wealth journey, may these parting words serve as a light of inspiration and empowerment:

Embrace the Journey:

Trust in your capacity to negotiate the challenges of wealth-building. Every move you make adds to the melody of your financial tale. Embrace the path with the bravery to learn from both accomplishments and problems, realizing that each experience changes your knowledge of sustainable prosperity.

Define Your Purpose:

Take the time to identify your purpose in generating money. Your objectives and ideals will drive your choices and imbue your path with significance. Ensure that your financial ambitions connect with your basic values, producing a feeling of purpose that transcends monetary rewards.

Cultivate a Positive Mindset:

Cultivate a positive mentality that fosters optimism and resilience. Acknowledge that setbacks are part of the journey and possibilities for progress. Use affirmations to reaffirm your conviction in your potential to build lasting prosperity, promoting a mentality of plenty and success.

Continual Learning:

Approach wealth-building with a spirit of inquiry and flexibility. The landscape of finance develops, and your dedication to ongoing learning prepares you for long-term success. Actively seek information from many sources, realizing that wisdom comes from a wide grasp of financial concepts, market trends, and personal growth.

Balance Your Priorities:

Strive for harmony in balancing your financial objectives with other concerns in life. A holistic approach guarantees that prosperity contributes to total well-being and satisfaction. Regularly reflect on your priorities, altering your money plan to match the ever-changing features of your life.

Courageous Decision-Making:

Approach financial choices with a combination of boldness and educated judgment. Consult with professionals as required, but follow your instincts as you travel your unique route. View measured risks not as impediments but as chances for development and success.

Integrate Contribution and Fulfillment:

Integrate contribution to society and personal satisfaction into your riches path. Recognize the enormous effect of giving back and donating to causes that connect with your beliefs. Envision your legacy as a tapestry woven with strands of both financial achievement and meaningful accomplishments.

Celebrate Milestones:

Celebrate your milestones, whether they be financial successes, personal progress, or constructive contributions to society. Cultivate thankfulness for the progress achieved, valuing the journey as much as the goal.

Create Your Symphony:

Understand that your path is a unique symphony, made with your values, experiences, and goals. It is a masterpiece that shows your originality and potential for great effect. Take the conductor's baton with confidence, knowing that you can construct your financial story with purpose and resonance.

Inspire Others:

As you grow on your wealth path, consider sharing your insights and experiences with others. Your observations may inspire and encourage people who go on similar journeys. Cultivate a legacy of mentoring and knowledge-sharing, contributing to a community of people empowered to develop sustainable prosperity.

As you begin on your path, remember that developing sustainable wealth is not simply about acquiring riches—it's about designing a life that resonates with meaning, satisfaction, and positive contribution. With confidence, purpose, and a dedication to holistic wealth, may your symphony be a masterpiece that resonates through centuries.

Dear Readers

I hope this communication finds you well. I am reaching out to express my thanks for deciding to go on the path of "Pillars of Wealth" with me. Writing this book has been a labor of love, and I genuinely hope you found it instructive, motivating, and a great companion on your road to sustainable prosperity.

If you appreciated the book and found its contents valuable, I would be very pleased if you could take a minute to express your opinions via a review. Your comment not only means a lot to me personally but also helps other readers find the book and its themes.

amazon.com/author/jordanpenix

Thank you for being a part of this adventure. Your support is sincerely appreciated, and I look forward to hearing your opinions.

Warm regards,

Jordan Penix